BECOMING YOUR OWN THERAPIST

Practical, Effective Strategies
to Manage Your Moods and Behavior

A Programmed Learning Workbook

Kevin J. Kelly, Ph.D.

GETTING THE MOST OUT OF THIS WORKBOOK

This workbook is intended to help you **become more independent in managing your moods and behavior**. The development of any new skill however, can be enhanced with the assistance of a teacher or coach. You may find that a therapist trained in Cognitive Therapy can be of significant help in mastering these techniques and others.

The workbook can be used in a variety of ways. You may find it most helpful to **review the table of contents** first to get an overview. Scanning the contents briefly may help you to get an even better idea of what is to come. You don't need to read the whole workbook to benefit from it. It was designed so that you could **read as little as one page at a time** and get something of value from that one page.

Beginning your reading with the first chapter will give you a sense of the approach used and the principles on which it is based. After gaining an overview and a foundation of understanding you may wish to go directly to the chapter which most interests you. The effectiveness of the technique you use depends in part on your skill in using it. You might find that setting **a few minutes** aside **each day** to read a chapter and do the exercises will allow you to gradually build your skill as you would with any new tool.

After you have reviewed the section called Thinking Mistakes (page 43) you will be able to use the Thinking Mistakes & Remedies section (page 46) to suggest the best techniques or remedies for dealing with that problem. It will be most helpful for you to **write directly in the workbook** in order to get the maximum effect or benefit. Later on you will be able to "think through" the problem using one or more of the strategies.

If you are fortunate enough to be working with a therapist you and she/he might find that a particular section is well suited to "homework" that you can do between sessions to further your progress. Just like in a psychotherapy relationship **you are in control** of what information is shared with other people. You may choose to share some, all, or none of what you write here. This commitment of privacy to yourself will allow you to be as open and honest as you would like in recording your thoughts and feelings.

PUBLISHER'S NOTE

The ideas and techniques presented in this workbook are not intended as a substitute for consulting with a mental health professional or your physician.

Send comments or inquiries to Kevin J. Kelly, Ph.D., Email: kevinjameskelly@gmail.com

TABLE OF CONTENTS

CHAPTER I
INTRODUCTION

This workbook contains a series of exercises which can help you to become more effective in managing your moods and behavior. It is based on a kind of treatment known as Cognitive Therapy. This kind of therapy helps people to feel better and behave more effectively. It is useful for a wide variety of problems. It is compatible with the use of medication prescribed by your physician and can even help your medication to work better.

Dr. Aaron T. Beck, one of the pioneers of Cognitive Therapy, often tells a story about the starving man who met a fisherman and asked if the fisherman would give him a fish. The fisherman said that he would do better than that, he would teach the man how to fish for himself. His reasoning was, if he gave the starving man a fish he could eat for the day, but if he taught him how to fish, he could eat for a lifetime. So it is with psychotherapy. A therapist can help us to feel better but if we don't acquire new skills we may find ourselves returning to the therapist every time we encounter a new problem.

This workbook can help you learn powerful strategies for dealing more effectively with anxiety, depression, and behavior/relationship problems. Research on the effectiveness of Cognitive Therapy suggests that when these strategies are used skillfully, people tend to feel better faster, and stay better!

The intention of this workbook is to help you progress from familiarity and knowledge to skill. The techniques which follow can be thought of as tools. As you become familiar with and practice the use of these tools, you can expect to get increasingly better results from them. As you become more skillful in your use of them, you may find that you begin to use them automatically and with less effort. Remember the difference between your first few bicycle rides and the one a year later? The overall result should be a general increase in your sense of well-being or peace of mind.

Your willingness to embark on this adventure will provide benefits which last a lifetime. Research studies show that by using the techniques which follow people can significantly reduce anxiety and depression. You may find that feeling better emotionally and making better decisions helps you to feel better physically and contribute to your overall health. Just as problems are passed from one generation to the next, so the strengths and wisdom you gain are a loving legacy for those who follow.

FEELINGS
(Emotions)

In order to know how to feel better, it is important to know how to identify what we are feeling on an emotional level. If we have learned to cope by ignoring feelings, they can seem strange or uncomfortable when we begin to learn about them. Emotions can be seen as a signal from our body that we can learn to understand and even benefit from. Research has shown that emotions result from two main factors: 1) thought processes and 2) biological changes resulting from those thoughts, or occurring independently of our thoughts. One researcher referred to emotions as *feedback from our organ systems.*

If we are going to become more effective in mastering our moods, then it will be important to be able to distinguish between feelings and thoughts. Most people and even many therapists are confused about this issue. Of course thoughts and feelings tend to be experienced together, but you will find that it is most helpful to make the distinction between your thoughts and your feelings. Here are some of the features of emotions:

- Emotions are usually experienced as a **physical sensation**. You may notice tension in your shoulders or a heavy feeling.

- Emotions can usually be expressed with **one word**, e.g., angry, sad, afraid.

- Emotions cannot be changed directly. They just exist. To change emotions we have to change our biology (as with exercise or a medication). We can also change our emotions by thinking differently.

Below are some examples of emotions and the situations they are related to.

Situation	*Emotion*
Lost job	Sadness
Awaiting results of lab tests	Anxiety

Please take a moment to write down some of the emotions you have experienced in the last several days and the situations they seem related to:

Situation   *Emotion*

___________________________   ___________________________

___________________________   ___________________________

THOUGHTS

An important step in learning how to change how we feel is learning how to change what we think. To do this, we must first learn how to identify what we think. Thoughts are basically representations of our internal and external experience. They may occur in the form of words, as when we silently talk to ourselves, or they may be visual images. They may even be memories of physical sensations. We can have thoughts intentionally or unintentionally. For example, see if you can picture a pleasant scene from a vacation you took. Good. Now see if you can recall what someone said to you earlier today. These are examples of intentional thoughts.

Unintentional thoughts are called automatic thoughts. They are different from regular thoughts in the following special ways:

- They are unintentional. They just pop into our mind.

- We may or we may not notice them. Can you recall one of the thoughts you had this morning as you were getting out of the shower? Were you aware of it when you had it?

- They may often be distorted. That is, not completely true. Have you ever thought to yourself, "this always happens to me?"

- They often lead to strong feelings (emotions).

Below is an example of a Negative Automatic Thought (NAT) which might be connected to the situation and feeling in the previous example:

Situation: *Lost job*
Feeling: *Sad*
Negative Automatic Thought (NAT): *I'm such a loser*.

Now become aware of and write down any NATs you might have had in relation to the situations and feelings you identified on the previous page.

Situation 1: ____

Feeling: ____

NAT: ____

Situation 2: ____

Feeling: ____

NAT: ____

THE COGNITIVE MODEL*

If our goal is to change the way we feel at certain times, it can help to be aware of what factors are influencing our feelings. The Cognitive Model is a kind of map of the human experience which can help us to see why we feel as we do. It is illustrated below:

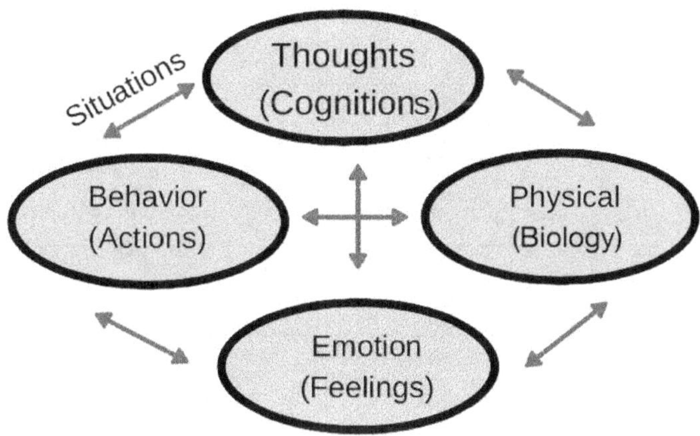

Here's how the model works. Thoughts, biology, emotions, and behavior can interact and influence each other as well as the situation. We encounter a situation or anticipate a situation. We have thoughts about that situation. If our thoughts are potent enough, they may trigger biological changes which we may experience as emotions (feelings). These emotions in turn may influence our behavior, which may have an effect on the situations in our environment. A more specific example might be:

>**Situation:** You pass someone in the hall and notice that they don't make eye contact.
>**Thoughts:** You have been friendly with this person in the past and remember that they usually greet you with a warm smile. You think that they are angry with you for something you said yesterday.
>**Physical:** Depending in part on your biological vulnerability, you may experience certain biological changes, such as fatigue.
>**Emotion:** You notice a sad feeling.
>**Behavior:** You avoid this person.

As the arrows in the model suggest, these factors can influence each other in almost any direction.

*Adapted from D. Greenberger and C. Padesky, 1990

COGNITIVE MODEL (CONTINUED)

Perhaps you can think of an example from your own life which illustrates the relationship between situations, thoughts, biology, emotion and behavior.

Situation: ____

____

Thoughts: ____

____

Physical: ____

Emotions: ____

How does your behavior affect the situation? ____

You may have noticed that some things in life can be changed more easily than other things. The Cognitive Model can give us more choices about how much influence we can exert on what, to change the way we feel. In other words, it can help to have some idea about the best things to change in order to feel better.

If we're feeling depressed (remember, we can't change feelings directly) we can change something about our biology, such as diet or medication. We can also change some aspect of our behavior, such as being more assertive in asking for what we want. Usually our decisions about what to change are better ones if we have looked at our thinking to make sure that it is accurate and useful.

The most important aspect of the Cognitive Model is that it offers us the opportunity to change the way we interpret our experiences, which can change everything else. The idea itself is a big change for many people who have seen themselves as only the victims of situations. Certainly, situations can have an effect on how we feel, but how we interpret those situations is a very powerful influence on how we feel and behave.

CHAPTER II
REDUCING TENSION & ANXIETY

Even the thought of anxiety can sometimes make us uncomfortable. What is this emotion and how can we put it to good use instead of being victimized by it?

Physically, anxiety is like fear. The main difference is that when we are afraid, we usually know what we are afraid of. With anxiety it may be a little more vague. We might notice sweaty palms or a racing heartbeat. Or we might find ourselves focusing on situations in the future over and over again. Sometimes we notice that we avoid certain situations or activities which really shouldn't be avoided.

When we feel anxious, we have sent a danger signal to our body which is intended to help us avoid harm. This can be very handy if we are outrunning a saber-tooth tiger but not very helpful when we're trying to get some sleep, or communicate with a spouse or a colleague. In a small percentage of cases, symptoms of anxiety may stem from of a medical disorder which can be successfully treated. The vast majority of anxiety symptoms are the result of negative predictions about the future. That prediction usually involves two general beliefs: (1) Something bad is going to happen and (2) we won't be able to do anything about it.

What are most people anxious about?
Research has shown that there are two primary areas of concern. One involves fears about physical health. The other involves fears about negative social consequences. When a patient discusses these issues with a cognitive therapist, they first explore the risks she/he perceives. By talking about fears in a safe, confidential setting, many people are able to quickly recognize the thoughts which are causing their anxiety. Cognitive therapists use a process called "guided discovery" which allows patients to identify thought patterns which trigger discomfort.

How can I make anxiety work for me?
We can start by understanding the meaning of our body's signals to us. Rather than a catastrophic interpretation of our sweaty palms or racing heart, we can understand that our body is trying to get our attention.

Five questions which can reduce anxiety.
Rather than automatically assuming that there is real danger, we can instead ask ourselves what thoughts or images have been going through our mind. One question many people find helpful is, **"What is the negative prediction you are making about the situation?"** Frequently this will help us to become more aware of the thoughts which are frightening us.

REDUCING TENSION & ANXIETY (CONTINUED)

Once we're aware of the negative predictions we've been making, we owe it to ourselves to consider the "upside" or the positive possibilities. Asking ourselves, **"What's the best that can happen?"** can help us to become aware of what usually is the opposite extreme. Take a moment to reflect on some of the things you have worried about and see how they tended to turn out. You may find that many things have turned out better than you thought. Mark Twain was quoted as saying, *I've had a lot of problems in my time, fortunately most of them never happened.*

Having examined the extremes of **what could possibly happen**, we can turn our attention to the probable. Many people suffer needlessly simply because they confuse the possible with the probable. It's possible for our house to fall down but because we don't consider it probable we dismiss that thought from our mind and feel comfortable about that issue. Asking ourselves **"What is most likely to happen?"** can help us arrive at a prediction which is likely to be more accurate than either of the extremes we have identified.

Remember that the second negative prediction we make when we're anxious is that we won't be able to cope with the bad thing that we fear. To test the validity of this belief we can ask ourselves the following question: **"Even if the worst happens, what could I do to cope?"** This can help us to update our awareness of resources for responding to problems. This is the time to get creative and come up with some possibilities you hadn't thought possible.

Finally, take or plan some action to influence the situation which you have identified as threatening. Rather than resorting to old ways of dealing with tension, ask yourself **"What are some steps I can take now, or soon, to positively influence the outcome of this situation?"** Again, time to get creative with this one. If you get stuck, ask a friend to help you "brainstorm" possibilities.

Make a list of those situations or worries that trigger anxiety for you:

____

____

____

____

The next exercise will help you learn how to reduce or eliminate anxiety when it is not helpful to you.

THE FEAR FORM
(Faster than a speeding Valium)

The following five questions will help you **reduce anxiety** by 1) identifying the negative predictions (NATs) which are contributing to your symptoms, 2) exploring the positive possibilities, 3) determining what is likely to happen, 4) identifying coping resources, and 5) planning action to influence the outcome.

Start by thinking about a situation that you feel anxious or fearful about and write it down here.

____

Example: *Lost job*

1. What is the negative prediction you're making about the situation?
This question can help you to become aware of the disturbing thought or image that is causing your body to feel those symptoms we call anxiety, i.e., sweaty palms, racing heart, tension, etc. Often there is a string of related thoughts, one leading to another more catastrophic than the one before. List as many as you can:

Example: *I'll never get a decent job. We'll have to sell the house.*
    I'll lose my family and end up homeless and disgraced.

Now write down some of the scary thoughts (NATs) that go through your mind when you think about your topic:

____

____

____

____

Rate anxiety level here:

   Calm —1—2—3—4—5—6—7—8—9—10—Very Anxious

Now turn the page and complete step #2.

FEAR FORM (CONTINUED)

2. **What's the best that can happen?** Now that you've explored the extreme possibilities on the negative end of things, how about looking at the extremely good things which can happen? Go ahead. You owe it to yourself. Don't skimp on this one.

Example: *I'll get an even better job with great pay and benefits.*

Now write down your best possibilities:

____

____

____

____

3. **What is most likely to happen?** Without doing anything different, what does all the evidence suggest will happen? Don't forget the difference between the possible and the probable. If there is little evidence to draw on for this situation, think of all the times in the past when you have predicted negative outcomes and review how accurate those predictions were. What percentage of those situations turned out as badly as you predicted?

Example: *It may be a number of months until I get another job, but it's not likely we will lose our house.*

Now write down what is most likely to happen in your situation:

____

____

____

____

Continue on next page and complete step #4.

FEAR FORM (CONTINUED)

4. Even if the negative prediction comes true, what could I do to cope?
Time to get creative! Using all your personal, financial, social, and
professional resources, how could you respond to such a challenge?
If you get stuck, ask a friend to help you *brainstorm* possible solutions.

Example: *If I don't get the kind of job I'm trained for, I could research*
other occupations and get trained. I could take a loan and start
my own business. We could live in an apartment for a while.

My partner could work more hours. We could live with friends
temporarily and share costs, etc., etc.

Now write down what you could do to cope:

____

____

____

____

This space is for notes or drawings to symbolize what you've learned so far:

Now turn the page and complete step # 5.

FEAR FORM (CONTINUED)

5. What are some steps I could take to influence the situation? There may be a number of things you can do now or in the near future to have an effect on the eventual outcome of the situation. Pretend you're helping a friend with the same dilemma. What would you suggest to someone you care about? If you took some of these steps, would it alter the probable outcome?

Example: *I can apply for unemployment. I can network with friends and associates. I can treat the job search like a job. I can identify my strengths and skills to see what other kinds of work I could do. I can do something that I've always wanted to do but couldn't because I had to work so many hours, etc.*

Now write down the steps you could take to positively influence the situation:

____

____

____

What ideas have been suggested by other people?

____

____

____

When could you begin to implement some of these ideas?

____

Now, rate how you feel **after** answering these questions.

Calm — 1 — 2 — 3 — 4 — 5 — 6 — 7 — 8 — 9 — 10 — Very Anxious

Now subtract your score here from your first anxiety rating as a measure of the degree of your success on this exercise. This is your anxiety reduction score.

FIRST RATING_____Minus SECOND RATING_____=_____Anxiety Reduction Score

THE FEAR FORM (SHORT VERSION)

Step 1. What is the negative prediction?

____

____

Calm — 1 — 2 — 3 — 4 — 5 — 6 — 7 — 8 — 9 — 10 —Very Anxious

Step 2. What's the best that can happen?

____

____

Step 3. What is most likely to happen?

____

____

Step 4. Even if the worst happens, what could I do to cope?

____

____

Step 5. What are some steps I could take to influence the situation?

____

____

____

____

Calm — 1 — 2 — 3 — 4 — 5 — 6 — 7 — 8 — 9 — 10 —Very Anxious

FIRST RATING_____Minus SECOND RATING_____=_____Anxiety Reduction Score

WHY WE WORRY

Two men were walking down the street. As they walked along the first man noticed that every so often the second man would wave his hand in the air. The first man thought that maybe the second man was just swatting flies (NATs?). After a few minutes the first man noticed that the second man continued to wave his hand in the air. Finally the first man couldn't stand the suspense any longer and asked the other man why he was doing that. The man replied, "That keeps the pink elephants away." The first man said, "There are no pink elephants around here." Without hesitation the second man replied, "See, it works!"

This silly story illustrates something very important about why we worry. In short we worry because deep down we think it helps. Just like the man who thought he was keeping the pink elephants away by waving his hand, some people actually find some comfort in worrying. That is, they think that by anticipating negative events which are very unlikely to occur, they are preventing them. A better explanation is simply that the things they worry about are not likely to happen in the first place.

Worry is our way of anticipating danger. It can be helpful to us as long as we don't get caught in an endless loop of focusing only on the negative prediction. When you notice that you are worrying about something, try using the Fear Form (page 9). Go through the five step process of discriminating between the possible and the probable. Then plan action steps to minimize the likelihood of the negative event while increasing the likelihood of the positive, or the best that can happen.

Don't Forget to Breathe

Controlled deep breathing can help to slow your heart rate and reduce other physical signs of anxiety. Try taking 10 deep breaths using your stomach muscles. The key is slow and steady. Practice this at least once a day. Then, when you notice that you are feeling anxious, try adding controlled breathing to your use of the Fear Form or any time you'd like to calm your body and mind.

CHAPTER III
MAKING BETTER DECISIONS WITH THE COST/BENEFIT ANALYSIS

The Cost/Benefit Analysis is a useful strategy for making decisions. Sometimes we make decisions that we are not even aware of. Depending on the choices we make, we can end up feeling bad unnecessarily. Or we end up choosing behavior which we regret. The Cost/Benefit Analysis can be helpful in making decisions about feelings, thinking and behavior.

Begin by recording the topic and date at the top of the next page. This will help you keep track of your thinking about certain decisions as you become aware of more information. Next, make a list of all the costs or disadvantages of a particular decision on one side of the page. A cost can be anything which has a negative consequence. It can be emotional, physical, financial, etc. Then list all the possible benefits or advantages of that same decision on the other side of the page. A benefit is anything which has a positive consequence.

Then rate each cost or benefit in terms of its importance to you on a scale of 1 (least important) to 10 (most important). Add up the cost column and the benefit column and the column with the most points is the winner. That is, it has more weight or significance than the other column. If you still feel indecisive about the decision, see if there may be a cost or a benefit you may have omitted. Still indecisive? Try the Fear Form (page 9). **Here's an example:**

TOPIC: *Continuing to think mostly negative thoughts about myself.*

Costs	How Important	Benefits	How Important
Makes me feel bad	9	*It's familiar*	5
I don't perform as well	8	*It's automatic*	4
I don't try as hard	7	*It's predictable*	3
I'm not as loving	8		
	Total: 32		Total: 12

DECISION: *It costs me too much to continue thinking such negative thoughts about myself. I'm going to give this workbook a chance to help me change.*

COST/BENEFIT ANALYSIS

Topic:____Date _____________________

Costs	How Important	Benefits	How Important
Total:		Total:	

DECISION:

____

____

____

CHAPTER IV
CONQUERING DEPRESSION

Most people experience depression at some time in their life. Sometimes we have days when we feel blue and we're not sure exactly why. If you're reading this, you've probably experienced depression in ways that interfered with your work, your family life or just your sense of well-being. The information and exercises which follow can help you to take effective action in becoming less depressed by changing the thinking and behavior which contributes to the problem.

Depression and Sadness

What is depression and how is it different from sadness? Sadness is a normal reaction to something which we interpret as a loss of some kind. Loss of a loved one usually triggers sadness, but a loss of self-esteem, or even a loss of hope, can have the same effect. Depression, on the other hand, is a syndrome, sometimes considered an illness which we experience as negative changes in our mood, thinking and our biology. We may feel sad (mood) and cry (behavior), more than usual. We may have negative thoughts about ourself, the world, and our future. We may feel listless and lack energy (physical). Depression which persists for weeks or more can be dangerous and should be treated by a mental health professional.

What Causes Depression?

Asking what causes depression may be like asking what causes water from our faucet. Is it the valve in the tap? Is it the water pressure from a pump or gravity? Or is it the rain which fills the reservoir? In the case of depression, we can point to our genetic vulnerability, our social or family situation, our behavior, or our thinking. Rather than trying to determine exactly what "causes" depression, it may be more helpful to point out the most effective ways to intervene and reduce the depression. There are several options: At the behavioral level we can increase our activity level. This has been shown to have a positive effect on depression. Your family doctor or psychiatrist may prescribe medication which changes your biology and can have beneficial effects on your mood. Cognitive Therapy tends to intervene at the level of thinking. As you will learn from this book and your own experience, changing your thinking can have powerful effects on your mood and behavior.

On the following page is a diagram which shows some of the symptoms of depression as they manifest in each area of our experience. Notice how they correspond to the areas described previously on page 5.

SYMPTOMS OF DEPRESSION

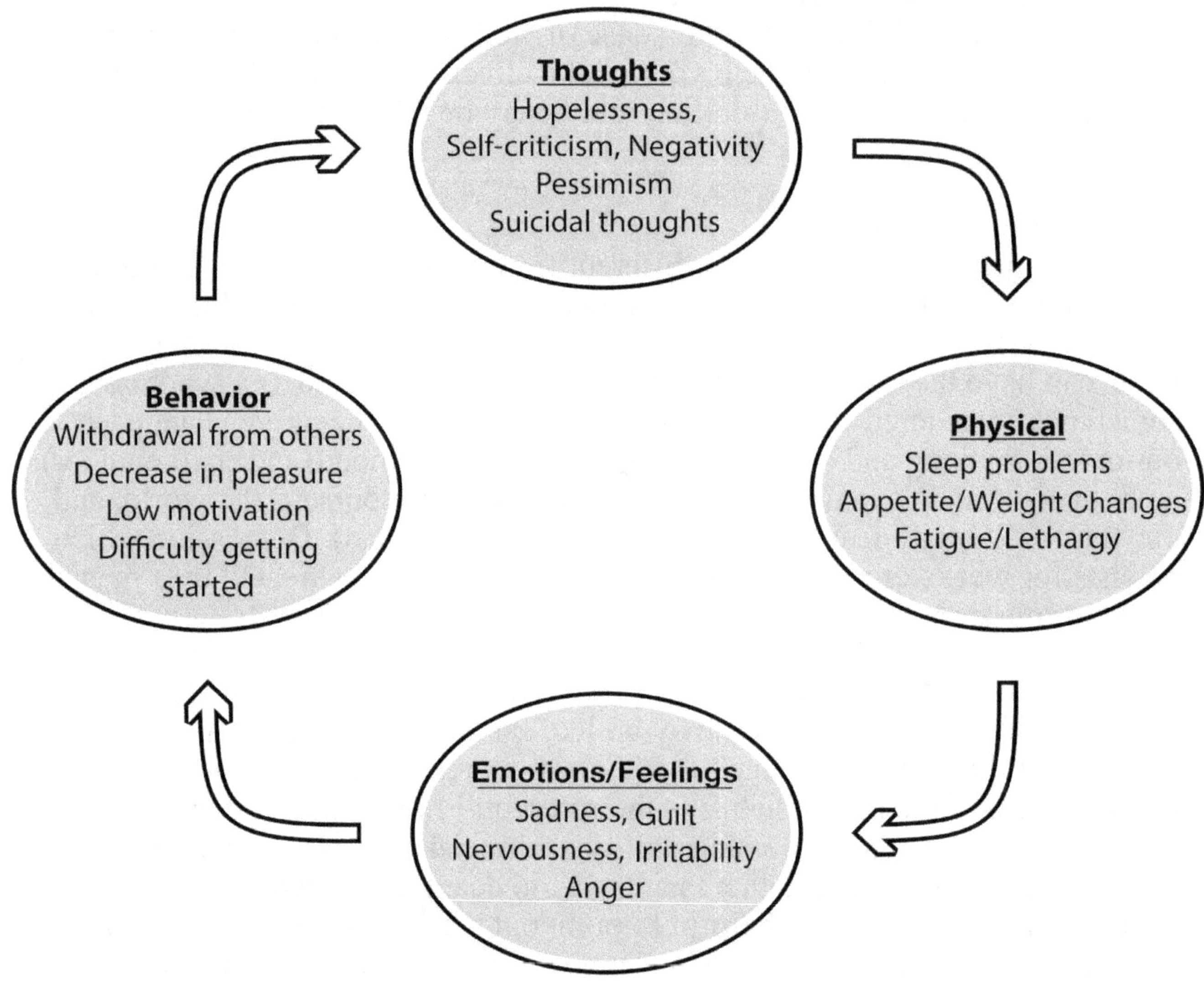

TAKING ACTION TO REDUCE DEPRESSION

Taking positive action is essential if we are to overcome the pain of depression. Although this workbook focuses primarily on changing our thinking, it is important to remember that physical activity can be a helpful part of feeling better emotionally and physically. **Increasing your activity level** under the guidance of your doctor is one way to take action.

Another way to take action is to **schedule pleasant events** which are distracting. Many people find it helpful to read an uplifting book or watch TV with a similar theme. Others enjoy events in which they can use a skill and tackle a manageable task. Volunteering or helping others in need is one of the most helpful forms of taking action; not just for the recipient but for you, the volunteer.

The ideas and exercises which follow can help you to reduce depression by changing the way you think. When you notice the sadness that so often accompanies depression, consider the possibility that there may be another way to think about the situation. This involves more than just positive thinking. One of the reasons why positive thinking may not have worked for you in the past is that it can be like trying to whitewash an old fence. If the surface of the old fence has not been properly prepared i.e., scraped and sanded, what will happen to the new paint? It will peel off. Similarly, positive thinking which is really not believed will not stick. Our old ideas will remain unexamined, and we will continue to believe that they are an accurate representation of the situation we are thinking about.

The next technique or remedy is called Testing the Evidence. This is probably the single most useful approach to changing depressive thinking. The other remedies are all related to this main strategy, the goal of which is to help you discover a "truer truth" about your situation.

A note about Negative Automatic Thoughts (NATs).
When you are working on changing a bad mood, make a list of all the thoughts which seem connected with that mood. Then identify the NAT which seems to have the most power to trigger that mood. Call this the "hot thought" and go after this one first. Since it has the most power to make you feel depressed, changing it can provide the most relief. If one thought doesn't seem to budge, try another. As your skill develops, you will begin to do the exercises in a kind of "mental shorthand" which will work much faster.

TESTING THE EVIDENCE

When we believe something, we tend to pay attention to information which supports that belief. We tend to see what we expect to see. If we are going to a party and expect that people won't like us, then we will tend to pay more attention to those cues that support or reinforce that expectation or belief.

Rather than swallowing hook, line, and sinker the negative thought as an accurate reflection of reality, we can examine the evidence on both sides of the issue. We can see if we might be overlooking some information which could alter the belief which is causing our emotional pain. Here's an example of how it works:

Situation: After her daughter got in trouble at school, a mother was feeling sad and depressed.

First identify the Negative Automatic Thought (NAT): *I'm a bad mom.*

Then, rate on a scale of 1-10 how strongly you believe this: 9

Now make a list of the evidence which suggests that the negative thought (NAT) is **true**:

Next make a list of the evidence which suggests that the NAT is **not true**:

True	Not True
My daughter got in trouble at school. *I yell at her occasionally.* *My husband and I sometimes fight in front of her.* *I don't help her with homework every night.*	*I really do care about her best interest.* *My neighbor said she was very well-behaved.* *I apologize when I make mistakes.* *I separate her behavior from her worth as a person.*

Now re-rate the strength of the NAT you have examined (1-10):   5

After considering all the evidence, what would be a more reasonable belief or way to think about this issue:

NEW BELIEF: *I'm not a perfect mom but I do some very important things for my daughter. I can plan some small steps toward becoming an even better mom.*

Following is an additional form for you to use to test the evidence in other situations.

TESTING THE EVIDENCE

Situation you feel badly about:________________________________

____

What emotion do you feel when you think about that situation?__________

Rate on a scale of (1-10) how strongly you feel that emotion: __________

Now identify the Negative Automatic Thought (NAT): ____________
____

Next, rate on a scale of 1-10 how strongly you believe this: ____________

Now make a list of the evidence which suggests that the NAT is **true**:

Next make a list of the evidence which suggests that the NAT is **not true**:

True	Not True

Now re-rate the strength of the NAT you have examined: (1-10) ________

After considering all the evidence, what would be a new way to think about this issue or what would be a new belief you could *try on*?

NEW BELIEF: ____

____

Finally, re-rate the strength of the negative emotion: (1-10) ____________

DISCOVERING HOPE

Sometimes when people are very depressed they have thoughts of ending their life. Some of those people even attempt suicide. If you are one of those people this section of the workbook will be very important for you. The one thing people who think about ending their life have most in common is a sense of hopelessness. That is they believe that things in their life which are troubling them can't improve or get better. The focus is on the future and the prediction is that not enough good will happen to justify their continuing to struggle.

Most people have a time in their life when they feel hopeless about something. Actually they are believing things are hopeless and that makes them feel sad. When we are totally convinced that we are helpless to influence a situation we give up and don't even try.

People who have hope on the other hand, believe that generally things will turn out okay. They also believe that even when things don't turn out okay there is something they can do about it. This second part is very important because often times we cannot control how things turn out but we can have a lot of control or influence on how we respond to those events.

If you are feeling hopeless please take a few moments to complete this section and talk to a health care professional (doctor, therapist, nurse) about your thoughts and feelings.

The exercise below can help to relieve the hopeless feelings and get you back on the road to health and well-being. Start by identifying the thoughts which seem connected to the helpless feeling.

If you are having serious thoughts about harming yourself please call the National Suicide Prevention Lifeline at 800-273-TALK(8255) or dial 911.

The following page will start you off with an example of the exercise.

DISCOVERING HOPE (EXAMPLE):

What are the negative predictions which are maintaining the hopelessness?

My life is ruined. I'll never get over this.

Notice that these thoughts are predictions. Because the thoughts are predictions you can use the Fear Form. Now ask yourself if you have ever had thoughts like these before?

Well, actually there was another time now that I think about it.

Remember in Step 3 of the Fear Form you asked What's most likely to happen? One way to figure out what is most likely to happen in the future is to ask yourself how these predictions turned out in the past?

Well, my life wasn't ruined and I did get over that particular problem.

You can also use Testing the Evidence (p.21) or step three of the Fear Form (p.10) so you can see the basis for your negative prediction.

Evidence that suggests the belief is: Evidence that suggests the belief is:

True	Not True
I've tried therapy before and it didn't help.	*I've never tried **this book** before.* *The Fear Form helped me to feel less anxious.* *I've never tried this new medicine before.*

Then you can go to steps four and five on the Fear Form (pages 11 and 12) to see what positive action steps you could take to improve the situation:

I could apply for assisted living. I could go to group regularly. I could take my medication regularly. I could learn to resolve conflict better.

OK, now it's time for you to try discovering hope. On the next page are the key questions used in the Fear Form. See how your answers can help you to feel more hopeful.

DISCOVERING HOPE

Step 1. What is the negative prediction(s) you are making which leaves you feeling hopeless?

____

____

Now rate your degree of hopefulness with 1 being least hopeful and 10 being most hopeful.

    Hopeless--1------2------3------4------5------6------7------8------9------10--Hopeful

Step 2. What is the best possible thing that could happen?

____

____

Step 3. What is most likely to happen?

____

____

Step 4. What are all the ways you could cope with the negative outcome you are predicting?

____

____

Step 5. What are some positive action steps you could take now or in the near future to influence the situation in the direction of the best possible outcome?

____

____

Now re-rate your degree of hopefulness after completing this exercise:

    Hopeless--1------2------3------4------5------6------7------8------9------10--Hopeful

Now subtract your first score from your second score to arrive at the progress score you achieved.

  SECOND SCORE_______Minus FIRST SCORE_______=_______Change in Hopefulness

Don't forget to work with other people on this exercise so that you get plenty of good ideas.

TAKING A SURVEY

Sometimes, even after we Test the Evidence, we still find that the old belief won't budge. This remedy can be a helpful way to gather more information about a belief you have which causes you pain.

We all take surveys informally when we notice how people react to us or even when we ask how someone enjoyed a dinner. It isn't always necessary to take a formal survey but sometimes it can be very informative to be direct in asking how someone sees us or what factors influenced someone to do something.

Donna realized that one source of her low self-esteem was the fact that she believed that she was basically a selfish person. As you can imagine this had a depressing effect on her mind, especially around occasions which involved giving and taking. Her cognitive therapist asked her if there was anyone she felt close enough to who she could ask about this issue. She stated that her friend Kathleen knew her well and might be willing to help. At the next therapy session she related with some excitement that her friend did not see her as selfish and listed off all the reasons why.

Interestingly enough, she said that because she did not see herself as a selfish person anymore she felt more comfortable asserting herself and asking for what she wanted. As a result of this she felt less resentful and found herself committing "random acts of kindness" more often. What effect do you think this had on the way people saw her?

Surveys can come in all forms. One man who was anticipating surgery was highly anxious about the outcome. By asking his surgeon about the percentage of fatalities resulting from this procedure, he was able to make a more accurate prediction of what was most likely to happen (see Fear Form on page 9).

As a result of the survey, he felt less anxious and was able to enjoy his loved ones without being preoccupied by death fantasies.

What are some surveys you could take to test the accuracy of your beliefs?

____

____

____

____

DEFINING TERMS

Defining terms can be a helpful strategy when you are using negative labels to describe yourself, someone else, or a situation.

Remember how you felt when you were a child and someone called you a name? You may have felt sad and may have sensed the injustice. Names like *jerk, idiot, loser,* etc. are not only destructive to us and others emotionally, but they are almost always grossly inaccurate.

Try defining what you mean by using the term *loser.* Does this mean someone makes mistakes more than 50 percent of the time? Does it mean that one tries but fails at something more than once?

Consider the failure record of Abraham Lincoln: He failed in business in 1831. Defeated for Legislature in 1832. Business failed again in 1833. Suffered nervous breakdown in 1836. Defeated for Speaker in 1838. Defeated for Elector in 1840. Defeated for Congress in 1843. Defeated for Congress in 1848. Defeated for Senate in 1855. Defeated for Vice President in 1856. Defeated for Senate in 1858. Elected President in 1860. Would you have called him a failure in 1859? Would that be an accurate description of this man?

Perhaps we humans can best be seen as a complex mix of strengths and weaknesses, hopes and dreams, failures and triumphs.

What is a negative label you sometimes give yourself? ________________

How do you feel when you do that? ________________________________

Can you define what that label means? ____________________________

____

Considering all the facts, what would be a more accurate description of yourself?

____

Perhaps our mistakes should best be considered as learning opportunities. Instead of calling yourself or somebody else names, think of what you can draw from the experience and plan how you will deal with a similar situation next time.

SHADES OF GRAY

The Shades of Gray remedy is a useful way of challenging all-or-nothing, black-or-white thinking. If we were limited to hot or cold as our only way of describing the temperature, we would be very limited in our choices of clothing. Because of this we would also find ourselves too hot or too cold much of the time. In the same way, overly simplistic descriptions of ourselves, other people, or even situations can rob us unnecessarily of self-esteem and opportunities for positive action. Here's how it works:

First you identify the Negative Automatic Thought (NAT) which seems like it has all-or-nothing thinking.

Example:NAT: *I'm a bad husband.*

Next, draw a line with 0 at one end and 10 at the other, like this:

0— 1 — 2 — 3 — 4 — 5 — 6 — 7 — 8 — 9 — 10
Bad   Good

Now realize that by using all-or-nothing thinking you have put yourself, someone else or a situation at one extreme of this Shades of Gray Scale.

Now see if you can think of what someone would have to do to really end up at that end of a Shade of Gray Scale. Perhaps someone who continually lies, cheats, or physically abuses his spouse might belong down there. Who would you put up at the other end of the Shades of Gray Scale? If you have already tried Testing the Evidence, consider the evidence that suggests that you are closer to *good* and mark the place on the Shades of Gray Scale where you would fit.

Try this exercise with an example of all-or-nothing thinking that you engage in.

NAT: ____

Think of extreme examples and write them under the 0 and 10.
0— 1 — 2 — 3 — 4 — 5 — 6 — 7 — 8 — 9 — 10

Considering all the evidence what would be a better placement on the Shades of Gray Scale for the issue you are considering?
What would be a New Belief concerning this issue? _______________

____

Following are additional Shades of Gray scales for you to evaluate other NATs.

SHADES OF GRAY

Negative Automatic Thought (NAT): _______________________________

____

Think of extreme examples and write them down under the 0 and 10.

0— 1 — 2 — 3 — 4 — 5 — 6 — 7 — 8 — 9 — 10

Considering all the evidence, what would be a better placement on the Shades of Gray scale for the issue you are considering?

What would be a New Belief concerning this issue? _______________

____

· ·

NAT: ____

Think of extreme examples and write them under the 0 and 10.

0— 1 — 2 — 3 — 4 — 5 — 6 — 7 — 8 — 9 — 10

Considering all the evidence, what would be a better placement on the Shades of Gray scale for the issue you are considering?

What would be a New Belief concerning this issue? _______________

____

· ·

NAT: ____

Think of extreme examples and write them under the 0 and 10.

0— 1 — 2 — 3 — 4 — 5 — 6 — 7 — 8 — 9 — 10

Considering all the evidence, what would be a better placement on the Shades of Gray Scale for the issue you are considering?

What would be a New Belief concerning this issue? _______________

____

THE BETTER EXPLANATION

The Better Explanation is a useful remedy for *Personalizing*, which is putting all the blame on ourselves or someone else for something we or they were not entirely responsible for. The classic example of this occurs when we are children. Children are in a constant process of discovering who they are. Because of this they tend to personalize many things which happen in their world. Research on the effects of the war in Bosnia suggest that children in that area believe that they are in some way responsible for the war. When children are abused or mistreated they automatically tend to assume that they caused the mistreatment. Some parents sadly reinforce this notion by saying things like "you deserved it" or "you're a bad boy/girl". The child then interprets this to mean "I'm bad."

As adults, we seem to continue this tendency in one way or another. If a loved one is angry with us we may think, "he/she doesn't love me" – "I'm unlovable (bad)." There is a **key question** we can ask ourselves which may shed a healing light in situations where we are personalizing. That question is **"Are there any other explanations?"** By asking this important question, we begin to examine the other factors which might help to explain the other persons behavior or the situation.

Let's try this question with the problem of the spouse who is angry. **"Are there any other explanations?"** Perhaps he is having a struggle at work and is feeling very frustrated about that. Perhaps she is feeling very threatened by a tone of voice which reminds her of how her father used to speak to her. Now, although we may have contributed in some way to the situation, at least we don't feel entirely (100 percent) responsible for it. Because we are not trying to defend against the possibility that we are bad, we are more likely to be able to problem solve with the other person.

Think of a recent situation in which you may have personalized what happened:

____

What upsetting thoughts (NATs) did you have?:_____________________

____

Now the big question. Are there any other explanations?: ______________

____

Following is a form on which you can record Better Explanations for five different situations.

THE BETTER EXPLANATION IN ACTION
(Quick Fix)

SITUATION: ____

NATs: ____

Better Explanations: _______________________________________

____

SITUATION: ____

NATs: ____

Better Explanations: _______________________________________

____

SITUATION: ____

NATs: ____

Better Explanations: _______________________________________

____

SITUATION: ____

NATs: ____

Better Explanations: _______________________________________

____

SITUATION: ____

NATs: ____

Better Explanations: _______________________________________

____

THE PIE CHART

Using a pie chart can help you to get a graphic representation of the situation you are reconsidering. It's particularly helpful as a follow up to The Better Explanation.

Here's the way it works: Let's say you have identified an automatic thought "I'm not good enough" and you have Tested the Evidence (p.21). You notice that much of the evidence (e.g., "Dad criticized me") which you have cited to support this belief (I'm not good enough) originated in your childhood. You may have actually come to believe that you were 100 percent to blame for your parents' behavior. The pie chart would explain Dad's behavior as follows.

Early explanation for
Dad's criticism:

After you do the The Better Explanation remedy, you realize that there were all sorts of other explanations for your parent's behavior, i.e., Dad was jealous of Mom's favoring you, you reminded him of his sister, he had no role model to learn positive parenting, etc. Here's how your pie chart might look with these explanations included:

Other explanations
for Dad's criticism:

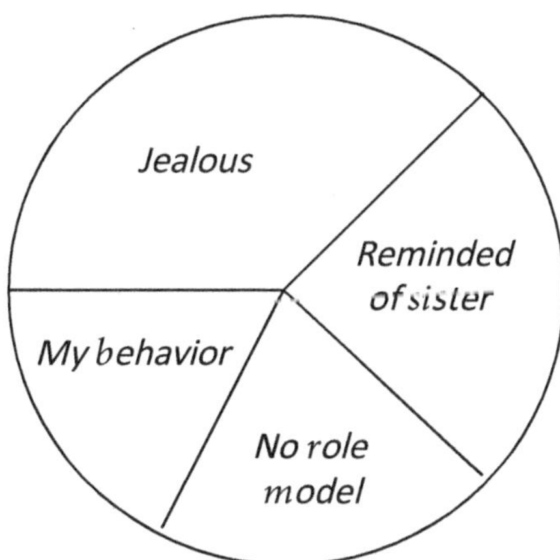

You can now see how different the picture looks with the other factors included.

THE PIE CHART (CONTINUED)

Perhaps you can think of a situation which you may be explaining in an overly simplistic way and would like to see represented more accurately.

Try putting the results of a Better Explanation here in Pie Chart form.

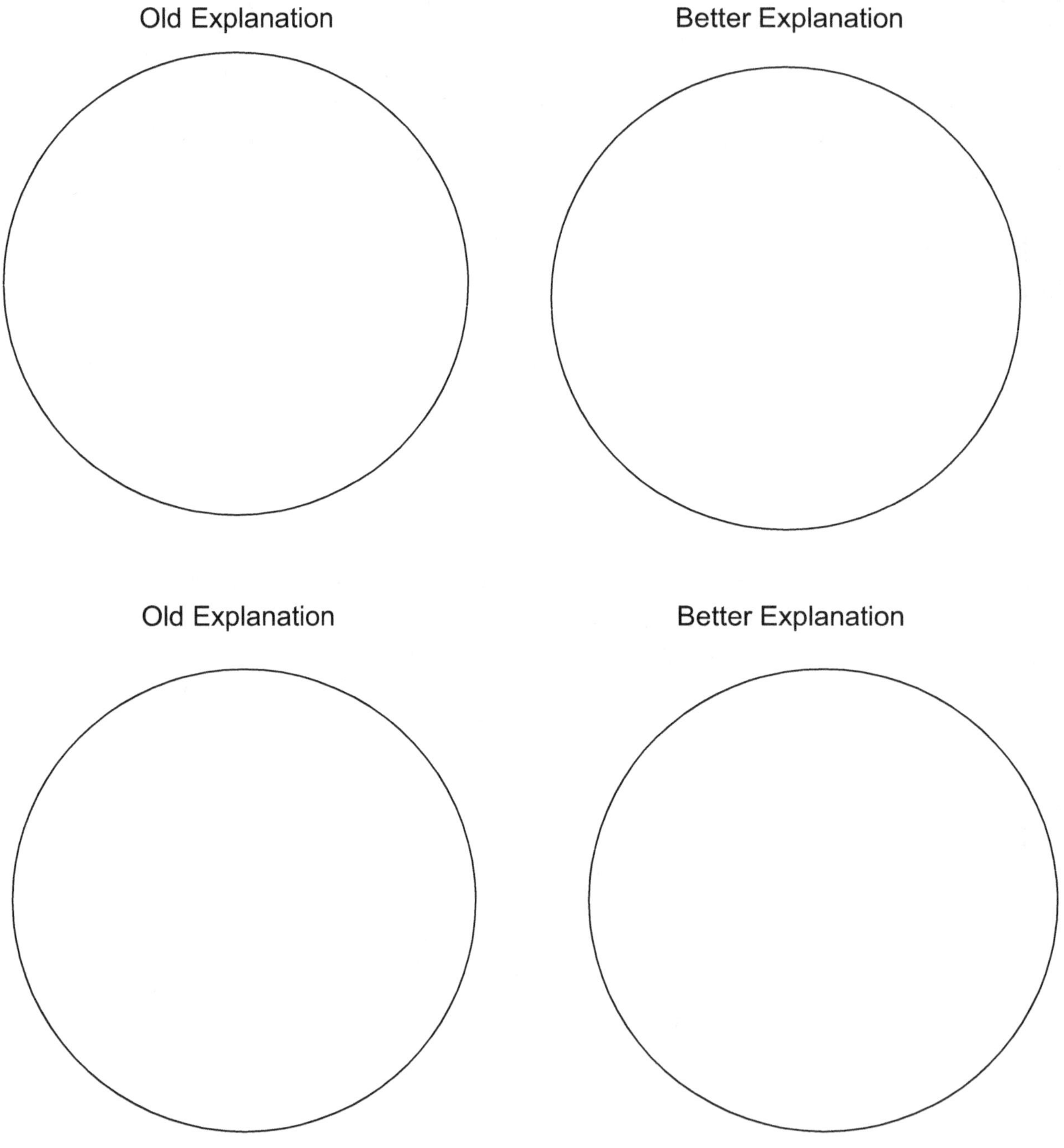

CHANGING PERSPECTIVES

This is a good way to get a different perspective on a difficult situation. If you were decorating a room, you could get different perspectives on the room by changing your position in the room. You could also change the location of the furniture to see how that affects the overall look.

With problem situations, you can do something similar by **changing the places of the players.** When you find that you are judging yourself harshly, imagine that you were talking to your best friend who was in your situation. Or when you find that you are judging someone else harshly, try putting yourself in his or her position. The saying "don't judge a man until you've walked a mile in his shoes" may be an earlier version of this.

Another variation of this technique is based on the Cost/Benefit Analysis (p.15). When you suspect that you may be giving too much attention to the negative aspects of a situation, try reversing the places of the positive and negative aspects and see how that would feel.

A man was going through a divorce and losing some property. His depression seemed directly tied to his focus on these losses. It was as though he was characterizing his life by the losses and assuming that they really were *terrible*. He was asked if he would be interested in looking at those and other losses or *liabilities* in his life. As you can imagine, he was able to identify a few others. We can always find what we expect.

Next he was asked if he would be willing to look at some of his assets, or the conditions which were present in his life which he valued. He began to list things like his car, his remaining properties, and other material items. He was asked how his vision was. He said it was good. Next he was asked how his children were. He said that they were fine and that he had a good relationship with them. He continued to add things that he appreciated and that he would not want to be without, e.g., feet, hands, best friends, his memory, his future, etc. It was suggested that he assign a value to each item from one to ten indicating the importance of that item. When he saw all the assets he had been taking for granted and how important they were to him, he viewed the losses differently. Finally he was asked to **reverse** the places of the assets and liabilities. How would he feel if he could gain back the losses but lose the assets? "No thanks," he said. "I'll take the losses."

Try this with some situations which are troublesome to you–kids, jobs, spouse, health, etc. Use the Cost/Benefit Analysis (page 15) when it seems to fit. Don't forget to include items you may be taking for granted.

Chapter V
Managing Anger & Conflict

How do you experience anger?

Anger can be a very upsetting emotion to have. Often we are left feeling shaky and flushed with our face locked in an angry scowl. You may notice tension in your muscles as you move and speak more quickly. More often than not we may regret something we have said or done. Benjamin Franklin was quoted as saying: *Anger is never without a reason, but seldom a good one.* Much of human tragedy has been fueled by this powerful emotion.

If it was unacceptable or unsafe to express anger when we were young we may find ourselves brooding silently or irritable. What is this feeling called anger and how can we make it work for us instead of against us?

Anger could have helped us to survive when we were living in more primitive times. Perhaps it's like our body's turbocharger in that it makes us stronger and faster. It's not too hard to see that it could help us to fight an enemy who was a physical threat to us or our family. One of the problems with anger is that when we get really angry our thinking gets very simple and we start to see another person as an "enemy" and suddenly the thought of hurting someone seems to make sense. Later after we have "cooled down" we are more able to see the situation in a different light and the person seems more reasonable and likeable. More like us.

How does anger work for us now?

How useful is it to express anger openly to another person? At first it can seem like the angry person is winning when she intimidates or gets in someones face. In that situation the angry person may get what they want just to calm them down. They may think that they have won, that the anger was useful. Afterward, however, the other person may feel resentful.

The recipient of the anger may not be very generous with the angry person in the future. Indeed we will probably try to avoid that person in the future. If we've been angry and harsh with someone close to us and they avoid us in the future, have we really won?

Of all the times you have been openly angry with another person how many of those times were you pleased with the outcome? Try the Cost Benefit Analysis (page 15) with anger to see if you gain more than you lose by expressing anger openly. How often did you wish you had handled the situation differently?

On the other hand, mild degrees of anger can help us to be more assertive with someone who is being aggressive with us. The challenge is to moderate our anger and behavior so that we get respect without resentment. The following example may illustrate the difference between helpful anger and destructive anger. Notice the thinking mistakes in the bad example.

Bad example:
What an idiot you are! (labeling, name calling). You only care about yourself (mind reading).

Better example:
John, I'm really angry that you didn't respect my sleep time by banging around. It makes me feel like you don't care about what is important to me. Is that true?

Anyone can become angry---that is easy. But to be angry with the right person, to the right degree, at the right time, for the right purpose, and in the right way---this is not easy.
Aristotle, The Nicomachean Ethics

The section on Win-Win Negotiation (page 42) will provide more ideas to make anger unnecessary in getting our needs met.

Angry Times

Perhaps this would be a good place to write down some of the situations which most frequently lead to anger for you.

1.____

2.____

3.____

4.____

3 Ways To Reduce Unhealthy Levels of Anger

Research suggests that most of the time the open expression of anger does not help to reduce it and in fact can make it worse. There may also be costs to our relationships. There may even be a cost to our health. There are better ways to deal with anger. In fact there are three primary remedies which seem to work best in reducing unhealthy levels of anger. One is to **question the thoughts and beliefs** we have about the offending person or situation. With higher levels of anger the best thing is to **distract yourself** while taking some time out from the situation and focus on things which are relaxing and pleasant. The third thing we can do with anger is to **negotiate** assertively with the person whom you are angry with. The section on Win-Win Negotiation (page 42) will discuss this technique.

It's Not Fair

Anger usually results when we believe we are threatened by someone's behavior or a situation. The threat may be physical but more often it is a threat to our sense of self-esteem, our dignity or our sense of fairness. We may sense that some important rule has been broken.

Name the Rule

What rule is being violated? Is it that "people shouldn't cut in line like that." Or that you should always get the attention and affection you deserve. Well, welcome to the club. Most people have had similar thoughts and feelings at some time in their life. Once you have identified the rule which has been violated ask yourself this important question; Well, if that's true, that the rule was broken what does that mean? Does it mean she doesn't love me or does it mean she's having a hard day. Another question we can ask is what does that say about me? That's where we usually find the Negative Automatic Thought (NAT).

Maybe this would be a good time to take a look at those situations you listed and write down some of the (NATs) you have about each one.

ANGER REDUCTION EXERCISE

Example:

SITUATION: *Husband/wife said, "hurry up and get in the car."*

Rule Violated: *My spouse should never be in a hurry with me.*

What does it mean? What does it say about me?

The answers to these questions are Negative Automatic Thoughts.

NATs: *He thinks he can push me around. I'm weak and helpless.*

Now do Changing Perspectives - page 33, The Better Explanation - page 29, or Testing the Evidence - page 20.

NEW BELIEF: *Maybe he/she is just anxious about the interview.*

There's plenty of evidence that I can be strong.

ANGER REDUCTION EXERCISE

Now you try it with some of the situations you listed.

SITUATION 1:____

RULE VIOLATED:____

NATs:____

Now do Changing Perspectives, The Better Explanation or Testing the Evidence.

NEW BELIEF:____
• •
SITUATION 2:____

RULE VIOLATED:____

NATs:____

Now do Changing Perspectives, The Better Explanation or Testing the Evidence.

NEW BELIEF:____
• •
SITUATION 3:____

RULE VIOLATED:____

NATs:____

Now do Changing Perspectives, The Better Explanation or Testing the Evidence.

NEW BELIEF:____

Congratulations! You do good work! *(Try saying that to yourself.)*

Short Term Effort-Long Term Benefit

Sometimes the things we get angry about occur repeatedly so if we can gain a better perspective on these situations we will be rewarded many times over.

Too Angry to Talk?

When we are very angry it is important to use ***time out*** or distraction. As long as we are aroused by anger we are not likely to find good solutions to problems, only enemies. Taking a long walk or doing some activity which is pleasantly engaging can allow us to cool off long enough to write down our thoughts about the situation so we can find a better way to see it. What are some situations where you could make use of this *time out* strategy?

1.____

2.____

3.____

Time Out, Not Abandonment

Please remember that taking time out does not mean abandoning the person we are angry with. It simply means we care enough about that person and ourselves to approach the problem constructively instead of destructively. Tell the person that you just need some time to cool off and you'll be back to work on it with them. Maybe even set a time with them when you will return, such as fifteen minutes or half an hour. After we have done that we will be much more likely to find a good way through the problem. The next section on win-win negotiation will help you solve problems with other people more effectively.

Be Prepared

The Boy Scout motto is appropriate here because one of the best ways to deal with anger problems is to stop them before they start. By preparing for situations which may trigger anger we are less likely to behave in ways we'll regret. By thinking ahead we can plan ways of thinking and behaving which are more likely to result in positive outcomes for us and those we care about. For the situations you listed write down below some ideas for thinking and behaving differently which will change the outcome of those situations for the better.

____

____

____

____

____

Great! Now you might be interested in learning a new way to resolve conflicts with other people and reduce the likelihood that anger will arise. The following story, *The Two Sisters and the Orange*, illustrates a new way of resolving conflicts so that everyone wins.

A STORY ABOUT WINNING

Other ideas on anger and conflict:
The Two Sisters and the Orange

Donna and Kathleen were standing out on the front porch of their house. They were having an arguement about an orange. Both of them wanted the orange and that day at least, there was only one orange. Donna's position was, *I found the orange first so it's mine.* Kathleen's position was, *you got the orange yesterday so I should get it today.*

Soon their mother came along and hearing the arguement said, *why don't you just compromise and cut the orange in half?* So they did that and each went her own way somewhat satisfied but not really. Each still felt a little resentful that the other got *their* half of the orange.

The next day the girls were out on the front porch again and sure enough they were once again arguing about who was going to get the orange today.

This time grandma came along and encouraged them to sit down and discuss the problem. Grandma asked Donna, *if you got the orange what would you do with it?* Donna replied, *I'd make orange juice.* Grandma asked, *how would you do that?* Donna replied, *I'd cut the orange in half and squeeze the juice out of the pulp.*

Then grandma asked Kathleen, *and what would you do with the orange if you got it?* Kathleen replied, *I'd bake a cake.* Grandma then asked, *and how would you do that?* Kathleen replied, *first I'd grate the peel of the orange and put that into the batter.*

Grandma said, *Oh, I see! Well, how about this idea... suppose we juice the orange and give that to you Donna so that you can have your orange juice. Then Kathleen, we can grate the peel so that you can bake your cake.* The girls agreed to this proposal and felt they had both won. Whahoo! Like magic. Imagine what it would be like if we could resolve all our conflicts so well.

Commentary

Each was **taking a position** which would result in a loss to the other, a "win-lose" outcome. Of course nobody likes to lose, and when we do the resentment we feel weakens the relationship. Sometimes we even want a loss for the other person to balance things out. This is a form of coersion or manipulation to get what we want.

This is the traditional **compromise**. The problem with compromise is that we seem to be getting less than we really want. We still lose. That loss leaves us a little resentful and hungry to win next time.

Something as simple as **sitting down** can help to create a better atmosphere for resolving a conflict.

Here grandma is identifying the **underlying interests** of the girls. Notice how different the underlying interests are from the initial positions the girls took.

Finally, Grandma offers a **proposal** which addresses the underlying interests of both girls.

WIN-WIN NEGOTIATION

Write down the subject of your conflict____

Step 1:   Listen carefully to the other person to better understand his/her underlying interests. Partners underlying interests:_________________

____

Step 2:   Give some thought to what it is that you want in terms of your underlying interests. Your underlying interests:_________________

____

Step 3:   Offer a proposal which takes into consideration what both you and your partner want. Your Proposal:_________________

____

Step 4:   Consider *brainstorming* or coming up with multiple ideas which could satisfy both of you at this point. If your partner doesn't a) accept your proposal or b) offer a counter-proposal which considers what would be good for both of you, then **you** offer a counter-proposal which might work better. If your partner is still negative or passive in response then you might propose that he/she take some time to think of an idea which could work for both of you.

Treat your agreement as an experiment which you can try out to see how well it works. That way nobody feels like they have been locked into something that might not be good for them. After you try the new agreement try reviewing with each other to see how it went for each of you. You can incorporate your findings into your next negotiation.

What did you agree to do (or not do)?____

____

When will you meet next to discuss how this worked out for each of you?

____

Refine your agreement by going back through the steps as necessary.
Congratulations!

CHAPTER VI
THINKING MISTAKES

Thinking mistakes are inaccuracies in our thinking. We can think of our thoughts as representations of reality, like photographs. If we have a smudge on the lens of the camera, then the photo will not accurately represent what was in front of the camera. Even if the lens is clear and we take a picture of only part of an object, then the picture will not accurately portray the whole object. It is safe to assume that everyone makes thinking mistakes so please don't assume that you are hopelessly defective if you recognize some or all of those described below.

It can be very helpful to be able to identify mistakes in our thinking because once we have discovered the mistake, we will know better how to correct it and feel better. Identifying our thinking mistakes is like diagnosing the thought problem. A good diagnosis usually points the way to a helpful remedy.

Below is a list of nine common thinking mistakes with examples of how they might occur. See if you can identify one or more ways that you have been victimized by this kind of thinking.

1. All or Nothing (Black or White): This involves seeing things as though there were only two possible categories. Example: If a situation turns out imperfectly, you see it as a total failure. You forget to buy one item on a shopping list and think "Well, I really blew that trip." Can you think of an example of how you have used this thinking mistake? Try writing it down below.

Your Example: ____

____

2. Overgeneralizing: A negative event is seen as a never-ending pattern of defeat. Example: When shopping you notice that your check-out line is moving very slowly and think "Why do I always pick the slowest check-out line?"

Your Example: ____

____

3. Mental Filter: Seeing only the negative aspects of a situation while screening out the positive aspects. Example: You focus on a critical comment someone made while ignoring all the compliments you've received.

Your Example: ____

____

4. Jumping to Conclusions: Predicting things will go a certain way before you have the facts.

> **A. Mind Reading**: Assuming that you know exactly what someone is or will be thinking about you. Example: An acquaintance doesn't seem as friendly as usual and you think "He must be angry with me."
>
> Your Example:____
>
> ____
>
> **B. Fortune-telling**: Predicting that things will turn out badly and that you won't be able to cope. Example: Before going to a social gathering, you have an image of people reacting negatively to you and you assume that you will be devastated.
>
> Your Example:____
>
> ____

5. Magnifying or Minimizing: Overvaluing or minimizing the importance of a situation or certain information. Example: Even though you may be a good parent and spouse, you think that it's shameful to have been laid-off from a job. You get several job offers and accept one but think that doesn't make up for thc loss.

Your Example: ____

____

____

6. Emotional Reasoning: Assuming that how you feel is an accurate reflection of how things are. Example: If you are feeling anxious, you assume that something bad is going to happen.

Your Example: ____

____

7. Shoulds: You tell yourself that things *should* or *shouldn't* be a certain way. We do this with ourselves, other people, and situations. Variations of this can include *musts, have to's* and other imperatives which sound like they come from some external authority figure. Example: "You have to help me," "I shouldn't have done that."

Your Example: ____

____

8. Labeling: This is an extreme form of all-or-nothing thinking which can be damaging to our self-esteem and our relationships. Instead of simply acknowledging a mistake, we say "I'm such a screw-up" (substitute *loser, jerk, idiot,* etc.). Applying labels to others (e.g., "that S.O.B") will tend to blind us to other qualities which could benefit us in the relationship. Everyone has labels they tend to use often. What are some of yours?

Your Example: ____

____

9. Personalizing (Blaming): This thinking mistake creates enormous preventable suffering. This occurs when we hold ourselves responsible for something which isn't or wasn't entirely under our control. As children, we take much of what happens around us personally, including how we are treated. When a child is mistreated by a parent, she will tend to assume that she is somehow to blame and may see herself as defective. When this process is reversed, we blame someone else for a situation we have a part in creating. We do this as adults often without realizing it. Now we have a choice about becoming aware of this destructive thinking mistake. Most importantly we can change it! Example: An acquaintance passes you in the market without saying hello. You think, "I must have done something wrong."

Your Example: ____

____

____

THINKING MISTAKES & REMEDIES
(What to do once you've identified the mistake.)

All-or-Nothing (Black-or-White): Seeing things as though there were only two possible categories. *Remedies:* Shades of Gray–page 27, Pie Chart–page 31, Testing the Evidence–page 20.

Overgeneralizing: A negative event is seen as a never-ending pattern of defeat. *Remedies:* Testing the Evidence–page 20, Shades of Gray–page 27, Pie Chart–page 31.

Mental Filter: Seeing only the negative aspects of a situation while screening out the positive aspects. *Remedies:* Testing the Evidence–page 20, Changing Perspectives–page 33, Pie Chart–page 31.

Jumping to Conclusions:
   A. Mind Reading: Assuming that we know exactly what someone is or will be thinking about us.
   Remedies: Taking a Survey–page 25, Fear Form–page 9.

   B. Fortune-telling: *Remedy:* Fear Form–page 9.

Magnifying or Minimizing: Overvaluing or minimizing the importance of a situation or certain information.
Remedies: Changing Perspectives–page 33, Testing the Evidence–page 20

Emotional Reasoning: Assuming that how you feel is an accurate reflection of how things are. *Remedies:* Fear Form–page 9, Testing the Evidence–page 20, The Better Explanation–page 29.

Shoulds: Authoritarian commands which make us (or others) feel pressured, condemned, often guilty.
Remedies: Cost/Benefit Analysis–page 15, Fear Form–page 9.

Labeling: Calling yourself or someone else names. *Remedies:* Defining Terms–page 26, Testing the Evidence–page 20, Shades of Gray–page 27, Pie Chart–page 31, Taking a Survey–page 25.

Personalizing: Holding yourself or someone else entirely responsible for something you or they were not entirely responsible for.
Remedies: Testing the Evidence–page 20, The Better Explanation–page 29, Pie Chart–page 31, Taking a Survey–page 25.

CHAPTER VII
USING THE REMEDIES

INSTRUCTIONS: The purpose of this form is to **help you change painful feelings/emotions** by re-examining your thinking about certain situations.

First identify the feelings you have and their current intensity (1-10):
Sad:________Scared:_________Angry:_________Other:_________________________

Next identify the situation (imagined or actual) that those feelings seem to be connected to (who, what, where, when, how): ————————————

____

____

Now identify the **Negative Automatic Thoughts** (NATs) or images which seem connected to the situation and feelings. Circle any "hot" thoughts:

____

____

____

Next, identify any **Thinking Mistakes** (p. 43) you can find in the *hot* NATs:

NAT   THINKING MISTAKE

___________________________   ___________________________

___________________________   ___________________________

___________________________   ___________________________

Now **apply the remedies**: see Thinking Mistakes and Remedies (p.46) for each mistake and summarize the results here:

NAT   NEW BELIEF

___________________________   ___________________________

___________________________   ___________________________

___________________________   ___________________________

Finally, **identify the feelings** you had and their current intensity (1-10):

Sad:______   Scared:______   Angry:______   Other:__________________

APPENDIX: WHAT IS COGNITIVE THERAPY?

1. Cognitive Therapy is an **active, goal directed process** which helps people to learn how to understand and change thinking and behavior. Research has shown that when people learn Cognitive Therapy skills, they are better able to control mood swings which can lead to anxiety, depression, and anger.

2. Cognitive Therapy is a **collaborative process** between client and therapist. Cognitive therapists don't try to interpret reality or tell their clients how to think. Rather, they teach methods clients can use to discover for themselves the kinds of thinking which work best for them.

3. A primary goal in therapy is to help clients **understand the links between thoughts, feelings, biology, and behavior.** With guidance from the therapist, the client conducts real world experiments to test the accuracy and emotional consequences of certain thinking patterns.

4. Cognitive Therapy is **compatible with the use of prescribed medication** to maximize the effect of a comprehensive treatment program.

5. Cognitive Therapy involves three primary activities: **a) Education, b) Skill Building,** and **c) Problem Solving** during which the client actively applies strategies learned to the problems which brought them to therapy.

6. **Progress is measured objectively** during the process of therapy so that both client and therapist can have objective feedback about the degree of progress being achieved.

7. Cognitive Therapy is **not just** *positive thinking* but rather a process of reappraisal. Taking a *second look* at important events in our life often leads to a more balanced view of ourselves, other people, and our expectations about the future.

8. The **goal of therapy** is not to eliminate emotions. It is to limit the severity and debilitating aspects of depression, anxiety, and anger so that our emotions work for us, not against us. As this goal is approached, the client experiences a **more balanced range of emotions.**

REFERENCES

Burns, David, M.D., <u>The Feeling Good Handbook</u>. New York: Penquin Putnam, Inc., 1999. This is an additional resource for those who wish to further their skill development with Cognitive Therapy.

Goleman, Daniel, Ph.D., <u>Emotional Intelligence, Why It Can Matter More Than IQ</u>, New York: Bantam Books, 1995. This is an excellent book which focuses on the "neurobioscience" of our emotional life.

Greenberger, Dennis, Ph.D and Christine A. Padesky, Ph.D., <u>Cognitive Therapy: An Individualized Workbook</u>.

Greenberger, Dennis, Ph.D and Christine A. Padesky, Ph.D., <u>Mind Over Mood: A Cognitive Therapy Treatment Manual for Clients</u>, New York: The Guilford Press, 1995. This manual is a comprehensive guide for additional learning in Cognitive Therapy. (The current title is: <u>Mind Over Mood: Change How You Feel by Changing the Way You Think</u>.)

ACKNOWLEDGMENTS

I wish to express special thanks to the following individuals for their part in making this workbook possible: Aaron T. Beck, M.D. for his pioneering role in developing Cognitive Therapy and his encouragement, Karen Simon, Ph.D. for her expert guidance and generous support in the early stages of hospital testing this workbook, and, my wife, Candice, who's talent and generosity have made this work possible.

ABOUT THE AUTHOR

Dr. Kevin J. Kelly is a clinical psychologist who has been active in the field of mental health since 1966. He has conducted or supervised over 1000 Cognitive Therapy groups. He founded and directed a hospital based Cognitive Therapy program and has been a program consultant and trainer in the development of numerous hospital-based programs. He created <u>Becoming Your Own Therapist</u> as a community education course and conducted research on the effectiveness of such courses in reducing depression and anxiety. He has presented numerous seminars on Cognitive Therapy for professionals and was a panelist on group therapy at the World Congress of Cognitive Therapy in Toronto, Canada. He presented his research findings on the effectiveness of courses using this workbook at the first World Congress of Behavioral and Cognitive Therapies in Copenhagen, Denmark. Dr. Kelly is a licensed psychologist in both California and Colorado. He currently serves as Director of Integrated Behavior Health at Pagosa Springs Medical Center in southwest Colorado.